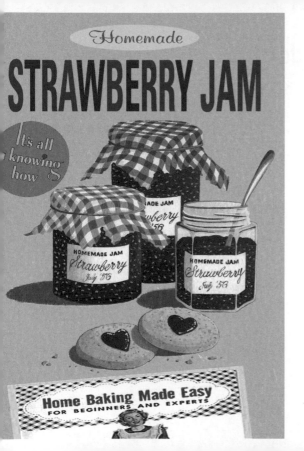

RETRO BAKING RECIPES

Favourite

*Delicious teatime treats
illustrated with
retro-style artwork by
Martin Wiscombe*

SALMON

Index

Printed and Published by J. Salmon Ltd., Sevenoaks, England © Copyright

Chocolate Brownies

4 oz. good plain chocolate   1 teaspoon baking powder
4 oz. butter   5 oz. caster sugar
2 oz. flour   3 eggs, beaten
4 oz. chopped mixed nuts

Set oven to 350°F or Mark 4. Grease and line an 8 inch square baking tin. Melt the chocolate and butter together in a bowl set over, but not touching, a pan of simmering water. Sift the flour and baking powder into a mixing bowl, add the sugar, pour over the chocolate mixture and mix well together. Stir in the eggs and chopped nuts and mix well. Put into the tin, spread out and bake for 25 to 30 minutes until a skewer inserted comes out clean. Leave to cool in the tin for 10 minutes, cut into squares and turn out on to a wire rack.

Home Baking!

SELF-RAISING
ENRICHED
Flour
BLEACHED
SPECIAL
NET WT 5 LB 12.26 '51

It was a piece of cake.

Victoria Sponge Sandwich

6 oz. soft margarine   1 rounded teaspoon baking powder
6 oz. caster sugar   3 large eggs
6 oz. self-raising flour   4 tablespoons raspberry jam
Caster sugar for dusting

Set oven to 350°F or Mark 4. Grease and base line two 7 inch sandwich tins. Put all the ingredients, except the jam, into a bowl and beat well for 2 minutes until smooth and blended. Divide the mixture between the tins and bake for 25 minutes until golden brown and springy to the touch. Turn out on to a wire rack to cool. When cool, sandwich the cakes together with a generous layer of jam and dust the top with caster sugar. If desired, a layer of whipped cream can be added with the jam.

Shortbread

4 oz. butter   6 oz. flour
2 oz. caster sugar   2 oz. ground rice

Set oven to 350°F or Mark 4. Cream the butter and sugar together in a bowl. Gradually sift in the flour and the ground rice, kneading the mixture into a ball. On a floured surface roll or pat the dough into a round, ½ inch thick. Place on a plain baking sheet. Pinch up the edges and prick the top with a fork. Bake for about 35–40 minutes or until firm and pale golden. While still warm, cut into triangles and sprinkle with caster sugar.

Cherry Cake

8 oz. glacé cherries, halved	6 oz. caster sugar
3 oz. plain flour	Grated rind of 1 lemon
3 oz. self-raising flour	3 eggs, beaten
Pinch of salt	3 oz. ground almonds
6 oz. butter, softened	Milk to mix

Set oven to 350°F or Mark 4. Grease and line a 7 inch round cake tin. Rinse the cherries, dry well on kitchen paper and toss in a little of the flour. Sieve together the flours and salt twice to mix thoroughly. Cream together the butter, sugar and lemon rind in a bowl until light and fluffy. Add the beaten eggs a little at a time, beating well between each addition, keeping the mixture stiff and adding a little flour. Fold in the remaining flour, cherries and ground almonds with sufficient milk to make a fairly stiff dropping consistency; this will help to keep the cherries suspended evenly. Put into the tin and bake for 1 hour 20 minutes or until a skewer inserted comes out clean. Leave to cool in the tin for 5 minutes then turn out on to a wire rack.

Plain Oven Scones

8 oz. self-raising flour
2 oz. butter
1 teaspoon caster sugar

¼ pint buttermilk, full cream milk
or soured milk
Pinch of salt

Set oven to 450°F or Mark 8. Grease and flour a baking sheet. Sift the dry ingredients into a bowl and rub in the butter. Add sufficient of the milk to make a moist and spongy dough. Turn out on to a floured surface and knead gently. Roll out to ½ inch thickness and cut into rounds with a 2½ inch pastry cutter. Place on the baking sheet. Brush the tops with milk and bake for 8–10 minutes until risen and light golden in colour. Cool on a wire rack. Serve split in half with butter and jam.

For rich scones add 1 beaten egg to the dry ingredients before adding sufficient milk. Brush the tops of the scones with beaten egg rather than with milk.

Madeira Cake

4 oz. butter, softened	A few drops vanilla essence
5 oz. caster sugar	8 oz. self-raising flour
2 eggs	Milk to mix
¼ teaspoon salt	3 slices citron peel

Set oven to 350°F or Mark 4. Grease a 6 inch round cake tin. Cream together the butter and sugar in a bowl until light and fluffy. Beat in the eggs, salt and vanilla essence a little at a time with a little flour towards the end. Fold in the remaining flour a little at a time with sufficient milk to produce a soft consistency. Put into the tin and bake for 50 minutes. Remove from the oven, arrange the slices of peel in the centre and return immediately for another 10 minutes or until a skewer inserted comes out clean. Allow to cool in the tin for 5 minutes then transfer to a wire rack.

Butterscotch Biscuits

8 oz. light brown sugar
4 oz. butter
1 teaspoon vanilla essence

1 egg, beaten
12 oz. self-raising flour
½ teaspoon salt

Set oven to 350°F or Mark 4. Grease or line a baking sheet. Melt the sugar, butter and vanilla essence together in a saucepan very gently over a low heat. Remove from the heat. When the mixture has cooled add the beaten egg and mix together. Sift the flour and salt into a bowl. Make a well in the centre and pour in the cooled egg/fat/sugar mixture. Knead into a stiff dough. This will be fairly dry, but it needs no extra moisture. Roll out to ½ inch thickness on a floured surface and cut out the biscuits with a 2 inch cutter. Place on the baking sheet with sufficient space to allow them to spread. Bake for 20 minutes until light golden in colour. Allow to cool slightly before transferring to a wire rack. Makes 20–24 biscuits.

TRADITIONAL
Chocolate Cake
CHOCOLATE
DELICIOUS & WHOLESOME

Chocolate Fudge Cake

CAKE MIX

8 oz. flour   2 oz. cocoa powder   1½ teaspoons baking powder   3½ oz. butter
7 oz. caster sugar   3 eggs, separated   ¼ pint milk   Almond essence
Icing sugar, for sprinkling

FUDGE FILLING

1½ oz. butter   3 oz. plain drinking chocolate   1 lb. caster sugar
¼ pint cream or evaporated milk   4 teaspoons vanilla essence

Set oven to 350°F or Mark 4. Grease a shallow 8 inch x 12 inch baking tin. Sieve together into a bowl the flour, cocoa powder and baking powder. In another bowl beat the butter with a wooden spoon until it is creamy then beat in the sugar and the egg yolks. Stir in the mixed dry ingredients alternately with the milk, a little at a time. Finally, add a few drops of almond essence. Beat the egg whites stiffly and mix in as lightly as possible with a metal spoon. Put the mixture into the tin, spread out and bake for 50 minutes to 1 hour. Transfer to a wire rack to cool. Prepare the fudge filling by putting all the ingredients, except the essence, into a heavy saucepan over a low heat. Stir gently until melted then bring to the boil and continue until the mixture begins to thicken. Add the vanilla essence, beat until the mixture thickens then set aside until cool. When almost cold, spread over the cake and sprinkle with icing sugar.

Chocolate Madeleines

4 oz. flour	4 oz. butter
1 level teaspoon baking powder	2 eggs
1 oz. cocoa powder	Apricot jam
4 oz. sugar	Desiccated coconut

Glacé cherries and angelica, to decorate

Set oven to 400°F or Mark 6. Well butter 10 to 12 individual, deep dariole moulds. Sieve together into a bowl the flour, baking powder and cocoa powder. In another bowl beat together the butter and sugar until creamy, then beat in each egg separately and then stir in the dry ingredients. Three parts fill each tin with the mixture and bake for about 15 minutes or until the cakes feel firm. Turn out on a wire rack to cool. Warm a little apricot jam. When the cakes are cold, brush each top and side with jam, holding on a skewer to do so. Then roll in the coconut and decorate the tops with half a glacé cherry and pieces of angelica.

All-in-One Fruit Cake

6 oz. soft margarine	1 teaspoon ground mixed spice
6 oz. granulated sugar	10 oz. mixed dried fruit
2 eggs	2 oz. glacé cherries, halved
2 oz. self-raising flour	1 tablespoon milk
6 oz. plain flour	Pinch of salt

Grated zest of 1 orange (optional)

Set oven to 325°F or Mark 3. Grease and base line a 2 lb. loaf tin. Put all the ingredients into a bowl and mix until thoroughly blended. Put into the tin and bake for 1 to 1½ hours or until a skewer inserted comes out clean. Leave in the tin to cool.

Chocolate Macaroons

1½ oz. cocoa powder	4 oz. ground almonds
3½ tablespoons milk	Vanilla essence
White of 1 egg	Rice paper
8 oz. caster sugar	Blanched almonds, split, to decorate

Set oven to 350°F or Mark 4. First warm the milk and dissolve the cocoa powder in it thoroughly. Whip the egg white stiffly in a bowl, fold in the sugar and ground almonds and then the cocoa/milk mixture. Lastly add a few drops of vanilla essence. Place rice paper on a baking sheet and spoon on equal size heaps of the mixture, according to preference, leaving room for them to spread. Top each cake with a split almond. Bake for about 15 to 20 minutes until cooked and lightly browned and then transfer to a wire rack to cool.

Look at the colours!
Macaroons

Home Baking Made Easy
FOR BEGINNERS AND EXPERTS

It's all in knowing how

Cider Cake

4 oz. butter	1 teaspoon cinnamon
4 oz. caster sugar	8 oz. self-raising flour
2 medium eggs, beaten	½ pint cider

Set oven to 350°F or Mark 4. Grease and line a 7 inch round cake tin. In a bowl, cream the butter and sugar together until light and fluffy. Stir in the eggs, cinnamon and half of the flour. Gradually add the cider to this mixture and lastly add the remaining flour and mix thoroughly. Put into the tin and bake for about 45 minutes until firm to the touch, golden in colour and a skewer inserted comes out clean. Leave to cool and turn out on to a wire rack.

Date Slices

8 oz. stoned dates
¼ pint water
1 teaspoon vanilla essence
4 oz. self-raising flour

4 oz. butter or margarine
1 level teaspoon bicarbonate of soda
4 oz. quick cooking oats
6 oz. caster sugar

Set oven to 350°F or Mark 4. Grease a shallow 7 inch x 11 inch tin. Chop the dates and place in a saucepan with the water. Bring to the boil and cook until soft. Add the essence. Sift the flour into a bowl, rub in the fat, add the bicarbonate of soda and stir in the oats and sugar. Put half the crumbly mixture in the tin and press down firmly. Cover with the dates, top with the rest of the mixture and press down. Bake for 20–30 minutes. Leave to cool in the tin and when cool, dredge with icing sugar and cut into slices.

Carrot Cake

8 oz. soft brown sugar   2 fl. oz. water   8 oz. carrots, peeled and grated
4 oz. raisins or currants   16 oz. flour   3 oz. butter   4 oz. chopped nuts
1 level teaspoon salt   1 level teaspoon bicarbonate of soda
2 level teaspoons baking powder   ½ level teaspoon mixed spice
2 level teaspoons ground cinnamon

Set oven to 325°F or Mark 3. Well grease a deep 7 inch square cake tin. Put the water, sugar, raisins, carrots, spices and butter in a saucepan over a low heat until the sugar has dissolved, stirring all the time. Then boil for 3 minutes. Remove from the heat and leave until the mixture is tepid. Then stir in the sieved flour, salt, baking powder, bicarbonate of soda and nuts. Mix well together. Place in the tin and bake for about 1 hour until firm and a skewer inserted into the cake comes out clean. Leave in the tin for 15 minutes to cool and then turn out on to a wire rack. Keep for 24 hours before serving sliced and buttered. This cake keeps well.

Picnic Slices

8 oz. plain or milk cooking chocolate	1 egg, beaten
2 oz. butter	4 oz. dessicated coconut
4 oz. caster sugar	2 oz. sultanas

2 oz. glacé cherries, chopped

Set oven to 300°F or Mark 2. Grease a Swiss Roll tin. Break the chocolate into pieces and place in bowl over hot water. When the chocolate is melted, pour into the bottom of the Swiss Roll tin and leave to set. Meanwhile, cream the butter and sugar together in a bowl and add the beaten egg, coconut, sultanas and chopped cherries. Mix well and spread evenly over the chocolate base. Bake for 30 minutes until golden brown. Leave to cool slightly in the tin then cut into slices with a sharp knife and transfer to a wire rack.

Date and Walnut Cake

CAKE MIX

8 oz. stoned dates, chopped   1 breakfast cup boiling water
1 teaspoon bicarbonate of soda   3 oz. butter   8 oz. sugar   1 large egg, beaten
1 teaspoon vanilla essence   10 oz. flour   1 teaspoon baking powder   ½ teaspoon salt

ICING

2½ tablespoons demerara sugar   1 tablespoon butter   1 tablespoon single cream

Set oven to 350°F or Mark 4. Grease and line a 12 inch x 9 inch tin. Pour the boiling water over the chopped dates and add the bicarbonate of soda. Let this stand. Meanwhile cream the butter and sugar together in a bowl. Add the beaten egg and stir in the vanilla essence. Add the flour, baking powder and salt. Add the date mixture to the cake mixture and mix well. Pour this runny mixture into the tine and bake for 40 minutes. When cool cover with icing and when set turn out or cut into slices.

Icing: Mix together the demerara sugar, butter and cream in a saucepan. Bring to the boil and boil for 3 minutes, stirring constantly. Cool a little and pour over the cake. Scatter with chopped walnuts.

Lemon Cake

4 oz. soft margarine   6 oz. caster sugar   2 large eggs   6 oz. self-raising flour
Grated rind of 1 lemon   4 tablespoons milk

SYRUP
3 rounded tablespoons icing sugar   3 tablespoons fresh lemon juice

Set oven to 350°F or Mark 4. Grease and bottom line a 2 lb loaf tin. Cream the margarine and sugar together in a bowl until light and fluffy. Add the eggs, flour, finely grated lemon rind and milk. Mix well to a soft, dropping consistency. Put into the tin, smooth the top and bake for 40 to 45 minutes until firm and a skewer inserted comes out clean. For the syrup, mix the sifted icing sugar and lemon juice together in a bowl and pour over the cake as soon as it comes out of the oven. Leave in the tin until completely cold.

Tea and Cakes

Cup of Tea 6d
Pot of Tea 9d
Cakes .... from 6d

Apple Scones

8 oz. wholemeal self-raising flour   1 teaspoon ground cinnamon
1 teaspoon baking powder   4 oz. butter   2 oz. soft brown sugar
2 medium sized cooking apples, peeled, cored and finely diced
1 medium egg

Set oven to 375°F or Mark 5. Mix the dry ingredients together in a large bowl. Rub in the butter, stir in the sugar and the diced apple and lastly stir in the egg. Mould the mixture into 10 or 12 heaps (as you would for rock buns) and place on a floured baking tray. Bake for 20–25 minutes. Cool slightly before transferring to a wire rack. Serve split, with butter.

Banana Cake

9 oz. self-raising flour
10 oz. sugar
4 oz. margarine, softened
3-4 ripe bananas, mashed
2 eggs

½ teaspoon salt
1 teaspoon vanilla essence
½ teaspoon bicarbonate of soda
Jam, to choice
Whipped cream

Set oven to 375°F or Mark 5. Grease and line two 9 inch sandwich tins. This cake is best made in a food mixer. Put all the ingredients, except the bananas, together into the mixer bowl and mix on medium speed. When blended stir in the well-mashed bananas. Turn into the two tins and bake for 25–30 minutes. Turn out on to a wire rack to cool. When cool sandwich together with jam and whipped cream. Alternatively this cake can be served plain.

This cupcake is mine

HOSTESS CUP CAKES 2 for 5d

How TO GET THE MOST OUT OF OUR Sunbeam MIXMASTER

Fruit Buns

12 oz. flour	3 oz. sugar
4 oz. ground rice	3 oz. currants
2 teaspoons baking powder	2 eggs, beaten
4 oz. butter	Milk

Set oven to 400°F or Mark 6. Mix the flour, ground rice and baking powder together in a bowl. Rub in the butter until the mixture resembles fine breadcrumbs, then stir in the sugar and currants. Mix in the eggs and sufficient milk to make a smooth firm paste. Turn out on to a lightly floured surface and roll out to 1 inch in thickness. Cut into 2 inch rounds and place on a greased baking sheet. Bake for 15 to 20 minutes until golden.

Seed Cake

6 oz. butter, softened   1 heaped teaspoon caraway seeds
6 oz. sugar   8 oz. self-raising flour
3 eggs, separated   3–4 drops of almond essence
   Milk to mix

Set oven to 350°F or Mark 4. Grease and line a 7 inch round cake tin. Cream together the butter and sugar in a bowl until light and fluffy. Whisk the egg whites in a bowl and then beat in the yolks. Combine gradually with the butter and sugar mix. Sprinkle in the caraway seeds and fold in the flour, adding the almond essence. If necessary, add sufficient milk to the mixture to make a thick batter. Put into the tin and sprinkle a few caraway seeds over the top of the cake. Bake for 1 hour or until a skewer inserted comes out clean. Leave to cool in the tin for 5 minutes then turn out on to a wire rack.

Flapjacks

8 oz. rolled oats
4 oz. butter or margarine

3 oz. caster sugar
2 tablespoons golden syrup

Set oven to 350°F or Mark 4. Grease an 11 inch x 7 inch baking tin. Gently heat the butter or margarine, sugar and golden syrup together in a pan until all are melted. Gradually stir in the rolled oats, combining well with the syrup mixture. Press into the tin and cook for about 20 minutes. Mark into fingers and leave in the tin to cool. When cold turn out and break up; the flapjacks should still be soft and moist.

Coffee Cake

CAKE MIX
6 oz. soft margarine   6 oz. sugar   2 heaped teaspoons instant coffee granules
1 tablespoon hot water   3 eggs, beaten   7 oz. self-raising flour
Pinch of salt   1 teaspoon baking powder

ICING and FILLING
4 oz. butter, softened   8 oz. icing sugar   1 tablespoon coffee essence
Chopped walnuts to decorate

Set oven to 375°F or Mark 5. Grease and base line two 8 inch sandwich tins. Cream the margarine and sugar together in a bowl until light and fluffy. Dissolve the coffee granules in the hot water. Beat in the eggs gradually, with a little flour with each addition. Sieve in the remaining flour with the salt and baking powder and fold in. Add the coffee mixture and mix well. Divide between the tins and bake for about 20 minutes until springy to the touch. Turn out on to a wire rack to cool. For the icing, mix the butter, sugar and coffee essence together in a bowl and blend well. Use to sandwich the cakes together and to cover the top. Finally, decorate with chopped walnuts.

Drop Scones

**8 oz. self-raising flour   ½ teaspoon salt   1 level tablespoon caster sugar
1 large egg   ½ pint milk**

Place the flour, salt and sugar into a bowl. Make a well in the centre and add the egg and the milk gradually, stirring to make a smooth, thick batter. Drop the mixture in tablespoons on to a hot, lightly greased griddle or heavy-based frying pan. Keep the griddle at a steady, moderate heat and after 2–3 minutes when bubbles show on the surface of the scones, turn over and cook for 2 more minutes. Place the finished scones in a warm, folded tea towel; this will keep them warm and by keeping in the steam will prevent them from drying out. Serve warm with butter and jam or honey.

Boiled Fruit Cake

4 oz. margarine	9 oz. self-raising flour
4 oz. soft brown sugar	1 egg, beaten
8 oz. mixed dried fruit	½ teaspoon salt
¼ pint water	1 level teaspoon mixed spice

Put the margarine, sugar, dried fruit and water into a saucepan, bring slowly to the boil and simmer for 5 minutes. Allow to cool. Set oven to 325°F or Mark 3. Grease and line a 7 inch cake tin. Put all the remaining ingredients into a bowl, add the cooled fruit mixture and mix to a thick batter. Place in the tin and bake for 1½ hours or until a skewer inserted into the cake comes out clean. Leave to cool in the tin for 10–15 minutes and turn out on to a wire rack.

TEA

Please

Village Fete
TEA TENT

Cup of Tea 6d
Pot of Tea 9d
Cakes .... from 6d
Lemonade 5d
Orange Squash 3d

"One lump or two?"

Chocolate Eclairs

¼ pint water	2 small eggs
1 oz. margarine	A few drops vanilla essence
Pinch of salt	Whipped cream
2½ oz. flour	Chocolate glacé icing

Set oven to 450°F or Mark 8. Grease baking trays. Put the water, margarine and salt into a saucepan and bring to the boil. Remove from the heat and add the sifted flour, beating well. Return to the heat and cook gently until the mixture leaves the sides of the pan clean. Remove from the heat, add the essence and beat in the eggs one at a time. Pipe the mixture on to the baking trays, using a plain vegetable pipe (the size of the eclairs depends on personal preference). Bake for 25–30 minutes. When cold, split and fill with whipped cream and coat with chocolate glacé icing.

Rich Plum Cake

8 oz. butter
8 oz. caster sugar
6 medium eggs, lightly beaten
8 oz. currants
8 oz. raisins
8 oz. sultanas

4 oz. glacé cherries, halved
8 oz. flour
8 oz. chopped mixed peel
8 oz. almonds, blanched and chopped
2 tablespoons rum or brandy
1 tablespoon black coffee

Set oven to 325°F or Mark 3. Grease a 9 inch round cake tin. In a bowl, cream together the butter and sugar until light and fluffy. Stir in the lightly beaten eggs one at a time with a teaspoon of flour after the third egg. Beat thoroughly. Mix all the dried fruit together with half the flour. Stir the rest of the flour, together with the peel and almonds, into the egg and butter mixture. Then add the floured fruit, the rum or brandy and the coffee. Put in the tin and bake for 2½ hours or longer until a skewer inserted comes out clean. To prevent the sides from burning, tie a band of brown paper round the outside of the tin before baking. Leave to cool in the tin and turn out on to a wire rack.

Treacle Scones

12 oz. self-raising light wholemeal flour
3 oz. butter   1 dessertspoon black treacle
½ teaspoon salt   7 fl. oz. milk, approx.

Set oven to 400°F or Mark 6. Add the salt to the flour in a mixing bowl and rub in the butter until the mixture resembles breadcrumbs. Stir in the treacle and enough milk to make a soft dough. Roll out gently on a floured surface to about 1–1¼ inches in thickness and cut into rounds with a 2 inch pastry cutter. Place on a greased and floured baking tray and bake at the top of the oven for 10–15 minutes. Cool on a wire tray. Serve the scones cut in half and buttered; they are delicious with lemon cheese.

Honey Fruit Biscuits

1 level teaspoon clear honey
4 oz. butter
4 oz. soft brown sugar
1 large egg

1 oz. chocolate chips
Grated rind of 1 orange
2 oz. finely chopped nuts
Pinch of salt

8 oz. self-raising flour

Set oven to 350°F or Mark 4. Grease baking sheets. Cream the butter and sugar together in a mixing bowl until soft. Beat in the egg and honey and stir in the nuts, grated rind, chocolate chips and salt. Sieve in the flour and mix well. Divide the mixture into balls each the size of a walnut. Place about 2 inches apart on the baking sheets and flatten slightly with a floured fork. Bake for 10–15 minutes until pale brown. Leave to cool for a few minutes and then transfer to a wire rack. Makes about 36 biscuits.

Great British
Biscuits

NICE

CUSTARD CREAM

Cakes

Biscuits

ROUND RICH TEA biscuits

BOURBON

"I want the Jammy Dodger!"

Viennese Tartlets

8 oz. hard margarine	2 oz. cornflour
2 oz. icing sugar	1 teaspoon vanilla essence
4 oz. flour	Lemon cheese for filling

Set oven to 375°F or Mark 5. Put individual paper cases into about 18 patty tins. Cream together the fat and sugar in a bowl until really soft. Sift in the flour and cornflour and add the essence. Mix well. Place a little of the mixture in each paper case and hollow out the centre. Bake for 20 minutes. When cool dust with icing sugar and place a teaspoon of lemon cheese in each tart.

Farmhouse Gingerbread

10 oz. flour
2 level teaspoons ground ginger
2 level teaspoons ground cinnamon
1 level teaspoon bicarbonate of soda
4 oz. hard margarine

4 oz. soft brown sugar
6 oz. black treacle
6 oz. golden syrup
2 eggs, beaten
¼ pint boiling water

Set oven to 350°F or Mark 4. Grease and line an 8 inch square cake tin. Sift into a large bowl the flour, spices and bicarbonate of soda. Melt the margarine, sugar, syrup and treacle together in a saucepan over a slow heat, then pour this mixture into the dry ingredients. Mix well. Stir in the beaten eggs and lastly add the boiling water and stir. Pour this runny mixture into the tin and bake for 40–45 minutes until firm. Leave in the tin for about 10 minutes then turn out on to a wire rack. This cake improves in flavour if kept for 48 hours.

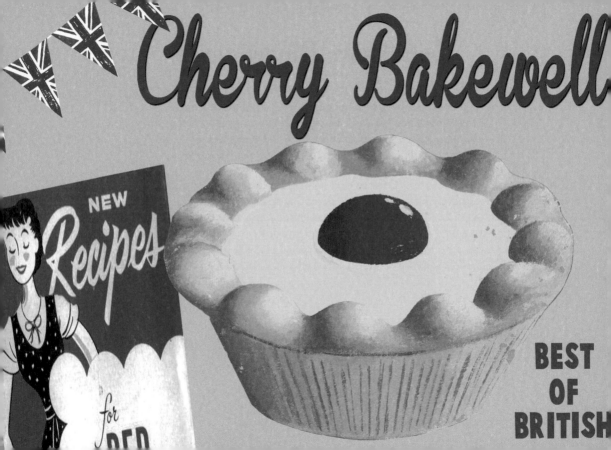

Lemon Tarts

BASE
3 oz. flour   2 oz. butter   ¾ oz. icing sugar   2 teaspoons cold water

FILLING
The juice of a small lemon   2 oz. caster sugar   1 egg   Icing sugar for dusting

Set oven to 375°F or Mark 5. Grease deep patty tins (makes approximately six tarts). Sift the flour into a bowl. Rub in the butter and add the icing sugar. Add sufficient of the water to make a moist dough. Roll out on a floured surface, cut into rounds and line the patty tins. Bake blind for 10 minutes. Remove from the oven and reduce temperature to 350°F or Mark 4. Meanwhile beat together the egg, caster sugar and lemon juice. Fill the pastry cases with the mixture and bake until set and the pastry is nicely browned. Serve hot or cold, but do not chill in the refrigerator.

Apple Cake

8 oz. self-raising flour   1 teaspoon salt   4 oz. butter, softened
4 oz. caster sugar   1 lb. cooking apples, peeled, cored and diced
1 medium egg, beaten   2 oz. currants
1 oz. chopped mixed peel   1 oz. demerara sugar for sprinkling

Set oven to 375° F or Mark 5. Well grease an 8 inch round cake tin. Sift the flour and salt into a bowl and rub in the butter until the mixture resembles breadcrumbs. Stir in the sugar, diced apple and egg and mix well. Add the currants and peel and stir in. Put into the tin, sprinkle the top with demerara sugar and bake for 30 to 40 minutes until golden and a skewer inserted comes out clean. Cool in the tin and turn out on to a wire rack. Serve, sliced spread with butter or, alternatively, serve warm with clotted cream as a pudding.

Dundee Cake

8 oz. flour	4 oz. sultanas
6 oz. caster sugar	2 oz. candied peel
6 oz. butter or margarine	1 oz. ground almonds
4 eggs	1 teaspoon mixed spice
4 oz. currants	1 teaspoon baking powder
4 oz. raisins	½ teaspoon salt

1 oz. split, blanched almonds

Set oven to 325°F or Mark 3. Grease an 8 inch round cake tin and line with greaseproof paper. Cream the fat and sugar in a bowl. Sift the flour, salt and spice together. Add the eggs and the flour mixture alternately to the creamed fat, beating them in well. Add the baking powder to the last of the flour. Stir in the ground almonds. Add the fruit and peel. Gently mix. Put into the tin. Arrange the split almonds evenly on the top of the cake. Bake for about 2 hours. After the first hour, if the top is browning too quickly, cover with greaseproof paper. Allow the cake to cool slightly in the tin before turning on to a wire rack. The cake will keep for several weeks if wrapped in kitchen foil.

METRIC CONVERSIONS

The weights, measures and oven temperatures used in the preceding recipes can be easily converted to their metric equivalents. The conversions listed below are only approximate, having been rounded up or down as may be appropriate.

Weights

Avoirdupois	Metric
1 oz.	just under 30 grams
4 oz. (¼ lb.)	app. 115 grams
8 oz. (½ lb.)	app. 230 grams
1 lb.	454 grams

Liquid Measures

Imperial	Metric
1 tablespoon (liquid only)	20 millilitres
1 fl. oz.	app. 30 millilitres
1 gill (¼ pt.)	app. 145 millilitres
½ pt.	app. 285 millilitres
1 pt.	app. 570 millilitres
1 qt.	app. 1.140 litres

Oven Temperatures

	°Fahrenheit	Gas Mark	°Celsius
Slow	300	2	150
	325	3	170
Moderate	350	4	180
	375	5	190
	400	6	200
Hot	425	7	220
	450	8	230
	475	9	240

Flour as specified in these recipes refers to plain flour unless otherwise described.